Having grown up on the mean streets of the English Riviera, Samantha Boarer started her poetry career in the internationally acclaimed post of Poet Laureate of Knowles Hill Secondary School. From there she migrated to Bath, where she studied creative writing and found her calling as a comedy poet. After co-founding Rhyme and Reason poetry events in Bath she moved to Bristol and began performing regularly in the South West. Having recently moved back to Devon, she intends to carry on funding her bohemian lifestyle by teaching impressionable youth at a local secondary school. Her (informal) research into what it means to be a 'real grown-up woman' inspires her to share her experiences with others in the hopes of helping them feel that they are not alone.

Real Grown-Up Women

Samantha Boarer

Burning Eye

BurningEyeBooks
Never Knowingly
Mainstream

This edition published by Burning Eye Books 2018

www.burningeye.co.uk

@burningeyebooks

Burning Eye Books
15 West Hill, Portishead, BS20 6LG

ISBN 978-1-911570-24-0

Real Grown-Up Women

CONTENTS

Skinny Girl 8
Stickly Flesh Thoughts 10
Love Is a Hipster 12
Real Grown-Up Women 14
Facebook Stalker 16
My Poems Will Make You Fall in
Love with Me 18
Love in the Cake Aisle 20
Google 22
Henry 24
An Offer Not to Be Missed! 25
Apology to My Vagina 26
The Curse of the Semicolon 28
Making Uncool Cool 30
I Want to Be 32
The Politics of a Short Skirt 34
Two Very Traditional and
Serious Haiku 35
Alright fer a Janner 36
Not a Love Poem 38
Pulling with Poetry 40
Sex Dream 42
To Netflix, with Love 44
Horse Issues 46
Instructions on a Break-Up 48
An Anti-Love Poem 50
My Current Poem 52

Tom Cruise's Front Right Tooth 54

SKINNY GIRL

I've got something to confess.

I used to have a twin,
but I ate her.
Mum was a bit annoyed at first
but then I told her,
'Shut it, or you're next.'

Because I'm a skinny girl
trapped inside a fat girl's body.
But don't worry, I've heard it all before,
and yes,
fat kids do sweat in cake shops.
Probably more so than nuns in sex shops,
but I'm no authority on that.

I have tried to find the skinny girl,
but excavation just isn't my thing.
And I've asked Time Team,
but they say the job's too big.

Some people even think I'm actually two people
wearing one pair of trousers.

The skinny girl always wants us to wear
these really awful skintight dresses.
She whispers in my ear, 'We look great.'
Then when I see photos of myself
I look like a sausage roll bursting out of the pastry.

That's not even the half of it.
Someone slapped my arse last week
and it's still jiggling now.

And the skinny girl is always hungry,
never stops eating.
You know when you go to Krispy Kreme,

and it says 'share a dozen'?
Well, technically I am sharing,
because there's two of us.

And the skinny girl
always tries to get me to do
ridiculous things like
jogging and… Zumba.

But I don't care if people call me fat.
I'm just a nutritional overachiever.
And I am 'in shape'.
A circle is a shape.

Anyway, I've lost the same
ten pounds so many times
that I think my cellulite is
getting déjà vu.

And I'm not too worried about
her getting the better of me,
because she's usually silenced
with a few slices of cake.

STICKLY FLESH THOUGHTS

I think about you constantly.
I think about you in the day, in the night.
I think about you like the day thinks about the night.

I think about you like salt thinks about pepper,
how we're not one without the other.
I think about you like crackers think about Cheddar,
how I'm so plain without your savoury goodness.

I think about you like stamps think about letters,
how I want to lick you all over,
and how I'm thinking Ronan's right,
love is like a rollercoaster
and I'm glad I'm as tall as the cartoon giraffe.
Old enough to ride you.

I think about you like spaghetti thinks about meatballs,
like bad films think about sequels,
like seagulls think about chips in the hands
of unsuspecting people.

I think about you like Scooby thinks about Shaggy,
how I'm usually a quivering mess
and you're not much better,
but I'm glad you're so unsteady, if a little sweaty.

I think about you like girls on Facebook
think about pouting,
like Jeremy Kyle thinks about shouting,
like Essex girls think about tanning
and maybe a little vajazzling.

I think about you like tone thinks about pitch,
how I'm a bit off without you.
I think about you like cream thinks about an embarrassing itch,
because, like an unsatisfied scratch,
I can't think of anything else.

I think about you like Ben thinks about Jerry,
how there's really no substitute.
I think about you how some women think about being hairy,
and how I know you wouldn't mind
if I was a little hirsute.

I think about you like nudists think about baring flesh,
and how I often think about you undressed.
I think about you like students think about being unprepared for
        tests,
but I don't know how to revise you,
so I just dive in with no regrets.

I think about you like
models are really thinking about McDonald's,
like my stomach thinks about somersaults,
like Daisy thinks about Donald,
and how your love has a stronghold over me.

I think about you like the day thinks about the night.
I think about you constantly.

LOVE IS A HIPSTER

Love is always trying to stop itself from saying,
'I prefer Love's original work,'
'I liked Love when it was more raw,' and
'I knew about Love before it was cool.'

Love is trying to go vegan and
consume only good and healthy things
even though you just want to stuff Love
with beef burgers and doughnuts.

Love likes to wear really oversized glasses
to make it appear smarter than it is.

Love likes to wear flower crowns
on its head to make it appear
sweeter than it is.

Love *loves* tea.
Love is all about herbal teas
and chamomile tea because
it's so good for keeping Love calm.
But don't ever give Love teabags.
It's all about loose leaf.

Everyone else's Love is 'pedestrian',
your Love is completely unique,
even though it constantly wears
mass-produced clothes from
Urban Outfitters that it 'customised'
by pinning an anarchist badge on to them.

Love also likes to raid your dad's wardrobe,
wearing his shirts from the eighties
because, you know,
dads were the original hipsters.

Love has just got into cycling
because it saves the planet and keeps you healthy.

But Love doesn't just ride any old bike.
Love rides a penny farthing
which it sourced from a fellow hipster
who swapped it with Love for seventy-nine pence
so that he could buy the premium version of Instagram.

Love Instagrams every inch of its life
so that everyone can see what a
great time Love is having,
even if the reality is that
Love is sitting at home every night
on the sofa watching old episodes of *Friends*
with only Ben and Jerry for company.

Love gets all of its clothes from charity shops.
Love says that other Loves have worn the clothes
and that every piece has a story to it
that maybe Love can soak up and learn from.

Love's flat is full of 'rare finds' and
distressed furniture that Love tells
everyone is from this little hidden flea market
that hardly anybody knows about…
when really it was from IKEA.

The last time Love dumped you
they told you it definitely was you
and not Love
because, well,
YOLO.

REAL GROWN-UP WOMEN

Real grown-up women buy their make-up from make-up
    counters.
They don't rifle through the bargain bin at Superdrug
looking for the least used tester lipstick.

Grown-up women don't accidentally grow penicillin
in their used coffee cups,
and they definitely don't tell a man who was flirting with them
about their dandruff of the face.

Grown-up women do not attempt to cut and dye their own hair
and end up looking like a cross between
a scarecrow and Boris Johnson.
They go to high-end salons and are treated like a princess
by an overpaid stylist
named after the country he was conceived in.

Grown-up women come out of that salon
looking like Kim Kardashian,
with a complimentary Kanye West
and a designer vagina to match.

Real grown-up women don't ask a room full of strangers
if they're the only one with a vagina acidic enough
to bleach their knickers,
or sing 'Born Free' every time they
come out of the shower freshly shaved.

Talking of vaginas, grown-up women get waxes.
They don't shave their own pubic hair
and walk around for a week
indiscreetly scratching themselves.

A real grown-up woman has a steady boyfriend
who brings her flowers, but isn't too clingy.
She doesn't get hit on by a drunk sixty-eight-year-old
who accidentally walked into a poetry show
and called her a 'very sensual vixen'.

A real grown-up woman doesn't
nap on a bed full of dishes,
doesn't have Super Noodles for dinner
or get chewing gum stuck in her pubic hair.
She doesn't do a twenty-minute poetry set
with a light shining up her skirt,
doesn't come on her period during sex,
doesn't stalk the fit guy who
works in Urban Outfitters
and definitely doesn't drunkenly tell men
she'll kiss them on the penis.

But, God, she must have a boring life.

FACEBOOK STALKER

It's hard being stalked by a stalker,
for that stalker to then stop being all stalky,
and you miss being stalked
and start to stalk your stalker.

It's hard at first when you're almost sure
your stalker is a murderer,
but even though he might be a psychopath
you're still too polite to tell him to bugger off.

It's hard when you do everything to throw him off.
Telling him you have a boyfriend –
oh, now I'm a lesbian –
actually, I'm a boy in a dress
and I married the Great Wall of China last week.

And then when I'd finally got rid of you
(you'd unfriended me on Facebook),
I wanted you back.

I wanted to sneak into your house
to smell your sheets.

I wanted to lick every bottle top
you'd ever put your dribbling mouth to.

I wanted to touch your spotty, pus-filled skin
and look into your dead grey eyes.

I suddenly knew what the songs on the
radio were saying.

I wanted to parade around in your
stained Y-fronts,
make a shrine to you,
put your image on a pillow
and steal locks of your greasy hair.

I would watch your Facebook profile for hours
to see what you were doing every minute of the day.

Then you added me again and I saw what a
weirdo you are and declined.

MY POEMS WILL MAKE YOU FALL IN LOVE WITH ME

My poems will make you fall in love with me,
and who said a girl can't laugh a guy into bed?
I laugh every time I see a man's penis.
It just makes them work harder.
My poems will make you fall in love with me
because I'm bloody adorable, if slightly unhinged,
and I know you love those jokes about my acidic minge.
So just be aware,
my poems will make you fall in love with me
and, girls, you're not safe either.
I've had more women's pants thrown at me than I've had hot
    dinners

My poems will make all of you want to take your clothes off as
    I speak.
My poetry will make my face appear on your lover's face
the next time you make sweet, sweet love,
and every time you think you're saying their name
you'll actually be saying mine,
because my poems will make you fall in love with me.

My poems will hypnotise you.
Look into the poems, deep into the poems,
not around the poems, into the poems,
not around the poems, into the poems.
My poems will make you fall in love with me
and everywhere you go you'll think you see me
out of the corner of your eye,
but when you catch up you'll realise
it was just someone who looks like me from the back
but isn't me.

My poems will make you dial my phone number
twenty times in one evening
but never actually call me.
My poems will make you try to message me on Facebook,

but all you'll be able to do is write 'I love you'
and delete it over and over again.

My poems will make the parents among you
wish I was your child and consider kicking yours out to house
    me instead.
My poems will make me everyone's weird crush
and make everyone who hears them awkwardly flirt with me
after.
My poems will make you talk about me all the time without
    realising,
until every sentence you say starts with my name.

My poems will make you realise you really have a thing for
chubby blonde girls with beef burgers for palms and sausages
    for fingers.
My poems will make you wonder
what other body parts I have that
you could compare to cuts of meat.

My poems will make you fall in love with me,
and every time you write a birthday card out for someone
you'll accidentally write it to me,
and you'll start writing poems,
but they'll all be acrostic poems using my name because
my poems will make you fall in love with me.

LOVE IN THE CAKE AISLE

Two thirty a.m. and I'm in Tesco's car park
in pyjama bottoms and the blazer I wore to work.

No one at home to ask about
my early morning shopping habits.
No one to criticise my two litres of ice cream
and bargain bin chick flick.

I see you first in fruit and veg.
Me by the bananas, you by the cucumbers.
I move away from the phallic foods,
they always get me hot under the collar.
Instead I stare at you until you glance my way.
I pretend to be looking intently at the magazines.
Your face looks puzzled from the corner of my eye
and I realise I'm looking at *Nuts* magazine.

We pass each other again in the cheese aisle
with the reduced section directly between us.
I start walking and you simply stroll.
There's a reduced chicken pie
and a broken sausage roll.
And as we both reach for the pie
I can feel the magic.
I almost say,
'You, me, chicken pie, marriage?'

But you change your mind
and carry on walking,
past the mincemeat and through into frozen.

Next we meet in feminine hygiene
and I wonder why you're there,
then you pick up some maxi pads
and I start to really hope your mum is incontinent.

Incontinence aside,
you look fit in the freezer lightbulbs,

and your maxi pads just make me want you more.
You walk past and drop something on the floor
and, on a single sanitary towel,
a note saying,
'Meet me, cake aisle, on the hour of four.'

GOOGLE

I've been noticing something creeping into my life,
a force much bigger than me, much more complicated.
It's taking over and I don't know what to do,
there's no one to protect me,
no charities, the police won't help
but I can't leave it myself.

Google is taking over my life. It owns me.
Everywhere I look, Google's there.
Even when I think I don't need help, it's there, telling me I do.
'Want to ask me a question?'
No, Google!
Okay, fine.

At first Google was clingy,
it made sure I wasn't using Ask Jeeves or, God forbid, Bing!
But after a while, I started using it even when I thought I
wasn't.
I used my Android phone – Google owns that.
Watching my favourite YouTube videos – Google owns that.
Writing my dissertation on Quickoffice – oh, hey, Google!

Google is hounding me,
it's reading my emails, recording my sleep patterns,
giving me advice on dating
but only showing results that make me nervous.
Google tells me I have a brain tumour when I just have a
headache,
and reads my blog on a regular basis.

All my documents are being shared with the world.
I even wrote this on Google Docs!

I don't need to go travelling any more because
Google Earth can show me what I'm missing.
I never get lost because Google Maps has got my back,
and I can even Street View my crush's house,
hoping they caught him undressing in his window.
Google has made stalking easy and accessible.

And I can't leave Google, I don't know a life without it any
    more,
and Google loves me, I know it does.
Of course it does me wrong sometimes,
but people don't know our personal
relationship with each other.
We have a bond I can't explain.

And I hear what you're saying.
'You can't have a relationship with a search engine.'
And to that I say, wake up, people, it's 2018!
Stop being so narrow-minded.

If I have a problem, Google's there to solve it.
If I need to share something with a friend, Google's got it
    covered.
There's enough of Google to go around, so I never have to be
    jealous.
But that's not enough for Google,
because it dreads the day I ever move to Yahoo.

HENRY

I loved you.
You were mine, and I was undoubtedly yours.
You'd never be with someone else,
you were just never that kind.
I loved your colour,
your vivaciousness,
your energy.

You could be the strong silent type too.
Sometimes you would turn your back on me,
but it only served to make me
love you even more.
I pined for you when you weren't around.

You were my best friend
and you always listened,
even if you didn't really have advice
or words of comfort.
We didn't need words, did we?
You always looked into my eyes
and it was like you knew
what I was thinking.
Friends didn't matter any more.
I could be myself around you.
You were a best friend
and so much more.

Then the day came when I saw you,
lifeless, motionless.
It was almost as if I could see you
floating up out of your body.

I sobbed like never before,
full of shock and unable to move.
I should have been there to save you,
to look after you.

You were a true friend
and the most loyal goldfish I ever had.

AN OFFER NOT TO BE MISSED!

Free to a good home,
one twenty-six-year-old, female,
kind-of-professional adult.
Fully house trained and
has a talent for folding fitted bed sheets.
Can only cook one nice meal,
but other meals include
'kackaroni cheese',
'chicken tikka lasagne'
and 'tuna korma'.
Comes with dark sense of humour
and questionable singing voice.
Bit guzzly on fuel but
overall a good little runner.

Collection only.
No returns.

APOLOGY TO MY VAGINA

This is an apology to you, my vagina,
and I'd love to look you in the eye
while I say this but
that's not physically possible.
So here goes anyway.

I've messed you about,
not been dedicated enough to you
or shown you the love you deserve.
But that stops now.
It's all candlelit dinners and
long sensuous bubble baths for you now.

It started pretty young,
after I realised I didn't just have a smooth bit
like my Barbies.
I was fascinated by you,
my fleshy little pencil case,
although I didn't try to stick crayons up you,
and I was too scared to touch you directly.
It was always through pants – vagina by proxy.

And I don't know how I found this out,
but I realised at about eight years old
that if I shoved a book hard enough
between my legs, it felt quite nice.

Now, you can't call yourself a book lover
unless you've masturbated with one.
Enid Blyton hardbacks were good,
but the sexiest book we owned was
the *Collins Family Encyclopedia*.

The first time I had an orgasm
it was an accident and I thought I was dying.
I was desperately trying to stop it
because I didn't want my mum to find me
dead with no knickers or trousers on.

I had no idea what an orgasm was
and I thought you might get pregnant from it,
and how was I supposed to tell my parents
I was pregnant at age eight?

I'm really sorry about all the hairstyles
(or lack of) I gave you.
Particularly waxing.
I felt like you had been ripped off.
I'm sorry about the time I let it grow and plaited it
because I thought it'd be funny.
It was just painful and nobody saw it anyway
because my housemates declined a viewing.

I apologise for comparing you to others,
or thinking you weren't normal.
I'm sorry for not doing enough kegels.
I know it wasn't your fault all those times
I laughed a little too hard
and a bit of wee came out.

But I promise to make you into
a vagina of steel in the future.

THE CURSE OF THE SEMICOLON

At GCSE we were wary of you.
You were intimidating,
but oh so alluring.
So out of reach of
our young illiterate hands.

We didn't see you often,
and when we did
it was an enigmatic glimpse
and then you were gone.

More common punctuation supported us,
but you were always there
lingering at the back of the classroom.

At A-level we saw more of you.
You were confident, cool,
and we wanted a piece of that.

Others came naturally to us
while you required some thought.
It didn't put us off,
just made you dangerous and enticing.

You tricked us into thinking
we understood you,
had surrounded you with the right words,
ignoring others for you.

We threw out the rules for you
while Full Stop halted in its tracks
and Exclamation shouted for our attention.

You followed us to university.
By now we were addicted.
You were on our minds day and night.

Your cousin, Colon, tried to warn us,

listed the reasons why
you were no good,
but you'd hypnotised everyone.

Our lecturers could see it was unhealthy
so tried to wean us from your charms.
We tried to justify it.
'You don't know Semicolon like I do;
he's different when it's just us.'

But even we could see
you were letting us down.
You'd started to come back
with red pen on you.
We started to see you in a different light
and decided that was it,
you wouldn't push us around any more.

It was hard to give you up
and now we don't see you so much.
We understand your ways more clearly now.
But if we ever feel that
old sense of weakening,
we remember the red pen you
came back with on your collar.

MAKING UNCOOL COOL

I'm making uncool cool,
so the more you tell me I'm lame, Mum,
the more I know I'm really cool.

I'm making social awkwardness cool.
Can't remember your name after meeting you five times?
No one minds because I'm that uncool kind of cool.

I'm so uncool cool I'm burning hot, like a,
like a burning hot thing.
I'm making going to bed at nine thirty cool,
because it's a school night and it's that
better get at least eight hours of healthy sleep kind of cool.

I'm that kind of uncool cool that makes you wish
you could be as uncool as me.

I'm that clumsy kind of uncool cool.
Almost broke my neck on a trampoline when I was eight
and almost broke my back on a bouncy castle at eleven.
My mum forbids me to go on bouncy things now,
which is why I'm not allowed to have sex with fat guys any more.

I'm making profuse sweating cool.
You're not with the in crowd if
your face, pits and backs of your knees aren't drenched.

I'm making that dishevelled look cool.
Not the carefully constructed kind of dishevelled, but the
I literally fell over three times on the way here kind of
dishevelled.

I'm the kind of uncool cool that rings my mum every day.
The kind that regularly overshares
but no one minds because I am hella uncool cool.

And who wants spontaneity?
I'm making all my potential lovers
go wild with my predictability.

Never straying from routine.
Oh yeah, that's right, I'm one hot predictable gal.

And flirting is never a problem when you're this uncool cool.
I've got heaps of stuff to say about the weather
and I could test anyone on the knowledge of motorways.

But let's face it,
none of you will ever be as uncool as me.

I WANT TO BE

I want to be your hair,
so that I could be stuck to you,
hugging your head
with my hairy arms.
Then when you go bald
you could keep me in a
shoebox in your wardrobe…
because I imagine that's what
men do when they go bald.

I want to be the cheese on your pizza.
Then when you take a bite of me
I'll turn into a long string of myself to tease you,
then some will be down your throat,
but the rest of me will still be on the pizza
because I won't want to stop
looking at your face.

I want to be your washing basket
so that when you throw
your dirty washing in me –
the shirt with the sauce spilled down it,
your old jeans with the hole in the crotch –
I can smell you.

I want to be the picture in the
frame beside your bed,
so I can watch you sleep.
You won't know I'm there,
but I'll be watching.

I want to be your toothbrush.
I'd rub myself all over your teeth,
while you swirl me all about
your lovely pillowy mouth.
I'd cover myself in your saliva
like a damp blanket.

I want to be your scarf,
so I can wrap myself
around your neck.

I want to be your shower
so I can wash your filthy body…
sorry, I'm getting too into this.

I want to be the mirror you look into
while you work out,
so I can see you all hot and damp.
Then I want to be the wall you lean on
so I can taste your sweaty, salty skin.

I want to be the food you eat
so I can run down your throat,
into your stomach,
so I can be inside you,
internally hugging your organs.

Anyway, let me know when you get this note.
Don't mind the mud on it.
I had to climb over that massive fence and locked gate
you've put outside your house.

THE POLITICS OF A SHORT SKIRT

I want to talk to you about something important.
Something that will resonate with a lot of people.
This is a subject I feel society has ignored,
so I implore you,
think of this as a plea for your empathy,
for the short skirt needs a spokesperson too.

For too long this problem been overlooked.
The short skirts of today are tired of discrimination,
and their determination to abolish their condemnation
is paramount in the normalisation of their hem location.

Not all short skirts want a life of being called slutty,
or having hands put up them, or eyes pierced through them.
They want to make friends with women's legs,
complement them in ways trousers could only dream of.
They want to make you feel good when they fit like a glove.

It's our right as women to enjoy our bodies.
It's not a short skirt's fault if
a woman is unwillingly accosted by a man's erection.

'Oh, but boys will always be boys,
real women should keep their clothes on.'
It seems the miniskirt's silence
is louder than a woman's objections.

The short skirt should be preserved as a tool of expression,
not an invitation to aggression.
Enough is enough, I say.
Let the short skirt live its days in peace.
Our skirts aren't there, 'sweetie', 'baby', 'honey',
for you to sink your teeth.

TWO VERY TRADITIONAL
AND SERIOUS HAIKU

People think I'm just
all about vaginas but…
actually, they're right.

At last, spring has sprung,
the birds sing in morning skies…
that cloud looks like a minge.

ALRIGHT FER A JANNER

Daggling over the ackers of vields,
'ee turned and looked dreckly to me eyes
and 'ee says to me,
'Maid, I ent never been one for
playin' urkey and mitchin' off,
and I ent no bibbler eever,
but yous one bowerly girl that's bin
leavin' me runnin' round like a cloppin' 'orse.'

An' I look at the buhy and the flickets
come to me cheeks and 'eeze got me thinkin'
that if us were ever to part
I'd bleddy miss the begger.

An' then we crocky down in the long grass,
I go daft as a brish, a proper doughbake like,
and sit there thinkin' 'ee's 'alf scat inn'ee?
But 'ee's proper 'ansome, so I don't much mind
if 'ee's mazed as a stoat.

An' then he goes to me again,
'Maid, I knows you ent no bint.
Why, you a helluva taffety girl to be going wiv
an' you ent got a brack about you,
an' I know yous as green as a dashell
and I'm glad of it too 'cos no buhy wants
to be eatin' up the orts.'

We lays there in the vield
an I think about dem uver buhys
bin bockin' me down and it's messed wiv me noggin.
An' I ask meself how I be ackin' now.

An' I thinks, yer, I'm aright as it goes,
an' this buhy 'ere next to me's aright an all,
fer a janner anyway.
An' tellin' the truth like, even when I were

just a tacker I couldn't o' dreamt of a nicer Demshir lad,
one that takes me on the grockle barges,
one that gets the oggys in whenever I fancy.

An' now I thinks I know what they mean when they say,
'Cousin Jack did'n know what thur legs was fer
till they looked over the Tamar an' seed Debn men walkin'
'bout,'
'cos when the zin titches th'eelz,
he be lookin' more of a man than I ever seen before.

NOT A LOVE POEM

I've never been one for big shows of emotion.
I don't like Valentine cards with gushy insides.
I like to keep my insides inside,
all my emotions in a little jar
that you can never get the lid off of.

But this poem is for you because, well,
I don't hate you, I think you're alright.
Out of a choice of you or a poke in
the fanny with a sharp stick, I'd choose you.
But they don't make cards that say that.

I'm not into hugging.
I do it mainly to be socially acceptable.
The word 'cuddles' makes me gag,
and not in a good way.

The thought of PDAs
makes me want to jump off a bridge
and in fact, I'd prefer people mistook us
for siblings rather than a couple.

But I will allow you to brush my hand
with yours around every two hours.
And you don't mind that,
you'll humour me.
If we get married, I bet you wouldn't
even mind having twin beds.

And I'll admit I have a commitment problem.
I make rubbish excuses.
I once dumped a guy for having a massive rucksack.
A second date feels like marriage to me
and I get scared.

But you don't mind if I don't call this a love poem.
It can be a like-you-very-much poem.

An 'I'm too emotionally inept to let you know
what I'm feeling' poem.
I'd start that genre for you.

You won't receive mushy love notes from me,
and I don't want that from you,
so have this
'I like you so much I'd give you my Wi-Fi password' card
because, you know,
I think you're okay.

PULLING WITH POETRY

I wish that poetry could help me pull.
I wish my similes and wordplay
could transform me from a short girl
with glasses too big for her face
into an exotic enigmatic woman with more
exciting curves than you can shake a circle at.

If only men would fall at my feet
every time I used astounding alliteration,
propose to me with every pop of onomatopoeia,
saying, 'You're the one metaphor me.'

The reality is,
short of tripping you up on your way to the gents',
I've never had men falling over
themselves to get to me.

So I thought I'd try poetry.
It works for guys, doesn't it?
At least, it did in medieval times.
I mean, Shakespeare was never short
of shorties up in his crib.

So far, it hasn't worked for me.
Maybe it's my skills that aren't up to scratch.
But I can spit a rhyme with the best of them,
I'll bowl you over with my hyperboles,
set your heart aflutter with my pace fluctuation.

But then it's downhill from there.
I mean, I can wow you with words,
but when I get offstage my idea of flirting
is asking you what your favourite type of bread is.
Mine's a wholemeal, gluten-free baguette, by the way.

And if you're thinking it can't be that bad,
think of Miranda Hart crossed with Ronnie Corbett.

But I'm more likely to tell you
that when I roll over in bed
my breasts clap
than make a clever wordplay joke about fork handles.

And to be fair,
writing poems about how I'd quite like to smell your
underwear,
posting them anonymously through your door
and throwing stones at your window
probably isn't the best way to go about things.
Some people have told me that's weird.
I thought you'd find it endearing.

So instead of hoping that
the words I speak indirectly to you here
will seduce you,
I'll just hedge my bets and embrace the weird to woo,
and say, 'I like baguettes, how about you?'

SEX DREAM

I had a sex dream about you
and, man, was it good.
We covered sexier things than a clitoral hood.
And now when I'm in bed about to fall asleep
all I can do is sigh and say, 'Oh, God.'
But not the good kind of 'oh, God',
the kind of 'oh, God' that asks
'why can't we do this in real life?'
Then I remember it's because
whenever I speak to you I say things
that involve clitoral hoods.

But we're totally on the same wavelength.
I mean,
you messaged me just as I was thinking about you.
Okay, so I was thinking about you non-stop for a week,
but I still call that fate.

And I don't think I can dream that vividly
about me doing that thing to your ear
without you knowing what went down
just a little bit.

I've even been dropping subtle hints to you,
like, 'Remember that time I put my mouth
around your whole ear and
just breathed really deeply?'

I know it was my dream but
how can you not remember that?
It was extremely erotic.

Maybe I'll just have to date you in my dreams.
But it might be hard to distinguish
between dream you and real you,
because, although dream you
never leaves me unsatisfied,

real you could probably still make me
orgasm just by touching my leg.

I've written a poem for you.
I'll read it to you one day.
It's got beautiful things in it.
It's also got really sexy things in it,
so I hope we get to the point where
I can stop waiting for you to fall asleep
before I climb in your bedroom window.

And I've thought about just telling you,
but what good will it do me?
Well, I'm fully expecting you to
drop whatever you're holding,
run through the mist
(there will be a steam train in the background)
and pick me up and swing me round
(you are much stronger in my dream).

And that's when you'll confess
your love for me.
And, although it probably won't happen that way,
it'll be okay,
because that thing you did in my dream
with your tongue and my elbow?
Well, that was really great.

TO NETFLIX, WITH LOVE

We met through my brother.
Just visiting, you only spent thirty days with us.
That was enough for me to fall for you,
madly in love with every TV show, film or documentary you
had.

We spent those thirty days in bed,
you showing me things I had never seen before.
You were the Lennon to my Yoko Ono.

University lecturers called for me,
employers vied for my attention,
but I only had eyes for the screen.

Your promise of exclusivity kept me interested.
I knew no one had what you had.
You were everywhere when I needed you,
on my TV, laptop and even my phone.
My bed filled with dishes and crumbs while deadlines
drew ever closer.

But then you had to leave.
You did it quickly, while I was asleep,
leaving nothing but a note saying
you wouldn't be some cheap fling.
All it would take would be £5.99 a month
and you'd be back in my arms.

Days, months, a year went on.
I graduated uni and things moved forward.
I got a job and could finally afford a TV licence
and stopped missing you so much.

Everyone around me seemed to be seeing you,
but I was already swimming in direct debits
and still couldn't provide you with what you needed
to stay with me month after month.

We'd see each other at mutual friends' houses
but I never got to see much,
so I couldn't keep up with your different episodes.
I just didn't know you any more.

So I decided to bite the bullet
and be the girl you needed me to be,
one who sits around in her pyjamas
with crusty pizza sauce stains on the duvet.

You are the most desirable of distractions,
perfect for procrastination.
I wait for friends to cancel plans so
that I can be back in the comfort of your arms.
I haven't gotten dressed for days
and that's absolutely okay by me.

HORSE ISSUES

Now, a lot of girls have issues
with the kinds of guys they date,
with certain figures in our lives
being varying degrees of present.

I don't want to get all Freudian about it,
but I've got issues.
Horse issues.
Yes, I date men who remind me
of the horse I never had.
The horse I fell off of when I was five
and never got back on.
Well, I've been on a few things since,
but I'm yet to find my stallion.

See, because I never had a horse,
it's given me issues Freud would
have a field day on.
Give me two men in a horse suit
and I'll have a good time.

It's just, I love men who can
feed off of the palm of my flat hand,
men who can fit a whole carrot in their mouth.
I've got reins and a harness
if anyone thinks they could be my equine prince.

I don't need a thoroughbred,
but bring me a Shire and I'll
grab him by the mane.

I'll call you whatever turns you on.
Oh yeah, horsey, yeah, don't trotting stop,
give it to me, horsey.

Be the horse I never had,
the pony I pine for,
the mustang I must have.

I love a man with a ponytail,
and obviously he has to be hung like a…
horsey men are just my thing.

And all I want is a man who can
jump over a seven-foot fence with me on his back.

Is that too much to ask?

INSTRUCTIONS ON A BREAK-UP

Step 1

Receive ominous text saying
'We need to talk'.
Apply waterproof mascara.

Step 2

Run out of the house,
forget to lock the door.
Tell self, 'I will not cry.'

Step 3

Struggle to see through the tears
let snot run into mouth.
Almost mow down swearing lollipop lady.

Step 4

Have sudden bout of nostalgia.
Picnics, skipping through meadows etc.

Step 5

Park haphazardly,
knock on door,
tell self, 'I will be calm.'

Step 6

Start shouting the second they open the door.
Accuse of cheating, say sorry, accuse again.

Step 7

Deny being a crazy person.
Ask why what you call passion

is enough to break up with someone.

Step 8

Switch wildly into self-blaming,
blow massive snot bubble and
shout, 'KISS ME!'

Step 9

Throw lamp at their head and storm out.

Step 10

Drive home.
Cry-sing to every song on the radio.

Step 11

Stop at shops.
Buy twenty-four sausage rolls, two tubs of ice cream,
frozen pizza and party pack for fifteen.

Step 12

Watch *Bridget Jones* in a sea of sausage rolls and vodka.

Step 13

Pass out on kitchen floor.

AN ANTI-LOVE POEM

I have something burning inside of me.
I want to shout it from the rooftops,
announce it on live television,
jump on Oprah Winfrey's sofa and shout,

'I'm not in love with you!'

I know it's that cliché 'girl leaves boy',
but I honestly can't wait to
start my life without you.

I mean, you know that feeling, right?
The one that makes you go all gooey inside?
The one where whenever I see your face
I feel physically sick.

Should I compare you to being struck by lightning?
You are more inconvenient and damaging.

I long to whisper sour nothings in your ear,
sweet insults and small threats.

I can't say it loud enough.
It excites me to the core.
I want nothing more than for everyone to know

I do not love you to the moon and back,
my heart doesn't jump at the thought of you and
my love for you is not like a raging river.

I do tremble at the thought of you,
but only because you anger me.
My hands do tingle at the sight of you,
but because I long to punch you in the face.

If kisses were raindrops
then we'd live in the Sahara.
If looks of disdain were water

then I'd send you to sea on a punctured dinghy.

I cannot convey how much I don't love you,
but here's a little poem just to try.

Roses are red.
Violets are blue.
I hope there's a pack of bloodthirsty wolves
outside waiting for you.

MY CURRENT POEM

My current poem looks at itself in the mirror.
'You're not as witty as the last one,
you could never live up to that.'

It cries a single tear and goes
to sit in the shower
to let the cold water splash over
its deflated ego.

Last week my current poem was the star of the show.
Warm and funny, the source of laughter.
Now it's something dark and dithering.
Something piercing has pricked
its self-worth and now it doubts
it was ever a poem at all.

Maybe she only had one poem in her,
my current poem thinks,
as it remembers being written,
sure that everyone would love it.
Maybe she was never a poet at all.

The current poem sits in my notebook
half-finished,
while its predecessor makes the rounds again,
until I can't perform without it burning a hole in my hand.

It writes 'ugly' in the condensation on the bathroom mirror,
whispers, 'She's only as good as my half-written self.'

Then I beat it down, strip it and rewrite
until I see something glowing.
It's my current poem, the same one, but this time
it's warm and funny like the last one.

And people are inviting me to perform
and telling me they love my work

and the current poem tells me
it knew I was a real poet all along,
it never doubted me and never will.

I go home carrying my ego like a giant weight
and lie in bed beside it,
hoping that it will still be there by morning
and that my current poem will be able to
morph itself into something new again.

TOM CRUISE'S FRONT RIGHT TOOTH

Sometimes I find the world
all a bit too much.
Adulting is hard when being a
cliché millennial is all too easy.
But at times like this I just repeat my mantra,
something that always
puts things into perspective for me.

Tom Cruise's front right tooth
is in the middle of his face.

As in, it is smack bang in the centre.
And if his front tooth can be
unapologetically central,
well, then I can surely get through anything.

If my rent is due but I'm a little short,
if I have a deadline at work
that I know I won't make,
or if that guy won't text back,
it's all okay,

because Tom Cruise's front right tooth
is in the middle of his face.

I'm not sure why Tom Cruise's
dental facts put me at ease with the world,
or why I feel so insatiable for
his right incisor.

But when I feel pressure from
people to get on with my life
(find a partner, have kids, buy a house),
I find immense comfort in
Tom's unusual ivories.

It's not his canines, wisdom or molars

or even that front left incisor
that bring me back down to earth,

but that central one, so right,
so pearly and white,
that makes life in general
just seem so absurd.

But should Tom ever feel the need
to correct this endearing trait,
I'm not really sure what I'd do.
I'd have to find someone with
something just as farcical
and pray that Will Smith
has toes as long as his fingers.

THANKS & ACKOWLEDGMENTS

Thank you to the family and friends who listened to all the rubbish jokes that didn't make it into this collection. I know it was painful

www.ingramcontent.com/pod-product-compliance
Lightning Source LLC
Chambersburg PA
CBHW032129050726
47590CB00008B/3021